How to Create a Comprehensive Five Year Financial Plan

Financial Planning, Volume 1

Karen Snow

Published by Roy Hendershot, 2024.

While every precaution has been taken in the preparation of this book, the publisher assumes no responsibility for errors or omissions, or for damages resulting from the use of the information contained herein.

HOW TO CREATE A COMPREHENSIVE FIVE YEAR FINANCIAL PLAN

First edition. July 15, 2024.

Copyright © 2024 Karen Snow.

Written by Karen Snow.

Table of Contents

Chapter 1: Understanding Financial Planning... 1

Chapter 2: Setting Financial Goals 4

Chapter 3: Budgeting for Success... 7

Chapter 4: Building an Emergency Fund 11

Chapter 5: Managing and Reducing Debt 14

Chapter 6: Saving for the Future 17

Chapter 7: Investing Wisely 21

Chapter 8: Planning for Retirement 25

Chapter 9: Protecting Your Wealth 29

Chapter 10: Reviewing and Adjusting Your Plan 32

Chapter 1: Understanding Financial Planning

Creating a financial plan is like mapping out a road trip. Imagine you're heading to a fun destination. You need to know where you're going, the best route to take, and what you need along the way. This is what a financial plan does for your money. It helps you figure out your financial destination, the steps to get there, and the resources you'll need.

A financial plan is essential because it provides direction and purpose for your money. Without a plan, you might find yourself drifting without a clear sense of how to reach your financial goals. Think of it as a GPS for your finances. It keeps you on track, alerts you to obstacles, and helps you adjust your course as needed.

There are several key components to a financial plan. These include understanding your current financial situation, setting realistic goals, creating a budget, saving for emergencies, managing debt, investing wisely, planning for retirement, and protecting your wealth. Each component plays a crucial role in ensuring your financial success.

A five-year financial plan is a roadmap that outlines your financial goals for the next five years and the steps you need to take to achieve them. It's long enough to make significant progress but short enough to adjust as your life changes. This plan will help you focus on what's important, make informed decisions, and stay motivated.

Having a long-term financial plan has many benefits. It helps you stay organized, reduces stress, and gives you a sense of control over your financial future. It also allows you to be proactive rather than reactive, which can save you time, money, and headaches in the long run.

There are many misconceptions about financial planning. Some people think it's only for the wealthy, but anyone can benefit from a financial plan. Others believe it's too complicated, but with the right guidance, it can be straightforward and even enjoyable. Finally, some think they can get by without one, but this often leads to financial problems down the road.

A financial planner can be a valuable resource. They have the expertise to help you create a comprehensive plan tailored to your needs. They can also provide objective advice and keep you accountable. However, you can also create your own financial plan with the right tools and knowledge. DIY financial planning can be empowering and cost-effective, but it's important to be thorough and realistic.

Setting realistic financial goals is the first step in creating a financial plan. Your goals should be specific, measurable, achievable, relevant, and time-bound. This means you need to be clear about what you want to achieve, how you'll measure your progress, ensure the goals are attainable, make sure they align with your overall financial picture, and set a timeline for achieving them.

Understanding your current financial situation is crucial. You need to know where you stand before you can figure out where you're going. This involves assessing your income, expenses, debts, and assets. It's like taking an inventory of your finances to see what you have and what you owe.

Assessing your income and expenses helps you see how much money you have coming in and going out each month. This is the foundation of your financial plan. You'll need to track your spending habits to identify areas where you can cut back and save more. This can be eye-opening and may require some lifestyle adjustments.

Budgeting is an essential part of financial planning. A budget is a plan for how you'll spend and save your money each month. It helps you live within your means, avoid debt, and save for your goals. There are different types of budgets, but the key is to find one that works for you and stick to it.

An emergency fund is a crucial part of your financial plan. It's money set aside for unexpected expenses, like car repairs or medical bills. Having an emergency fund can prevent you from going into debt when life throws you a curveball. Aim to save at least three to six months' worth of living expenses.

Debt can be a significant obstacle to achieving your financial goals. It's essential to understand the impact of debt on your finances and develop strategies to manage and reduce it. This might involve creating a debt repayment plan, consolidating debt, or negotiating with creditors.

Saving for retirement is another critical component of your financial plan. It's never too early to start saving for your golden years. There are different types of retirement accounts, each with its benefits and limitations. Understanding these options can help you make informed decisions about your retirement savings.

Insurance is an often overlooked but essential part of financial planning. It protects you and your family from financial loss due to unforeseen events, like illness, accidents, or natural disasters. There are various types of insurance, including health, life, disability, and property insurance. Choosing the right policies is crucial to your financial security.

Creating a financial plan may seem daunting, but breaking it down into manageable steps can make it more approachable. Start by setting clear goals, understanding your financial situation, and creating a budget. From there, focus on building an emergency fund, managing debt, saving for retirement, and protecting your wealth with insurance.

Regularly reviewing and adjusting your financial plan is essential. Your financial situation and goals may change over time, and your plan should reflect these changes. Set aside time each year to review your plan, assess your progress, and make any necessary adjustments.

A solid financial plan can give you peace of mind and a sense of control over your financial future. It allows you to make informed decisions, stay on track, and achieve your goals. Whether you're saving for a down payment on a house, paying off debt, or planning for retirement, a financial plan can help you get there.

Now that you understand the importance of financial planning and the key components involved, it's time to dive deeper into each aspect. In the next chapter, we'll explore how to set financial goals that are realistic, achievable, and aligned with your overall financial picture.

Chapter 2: Setting Financial Goals

Setting financial goals is like charting a course for a journey. You need to know where you're going and what you want to achieve along the way. Financial goals give you direction and purpose for your money. They help you focus on what's important and make informed decisions about how to spend and save.

The importance of setting financial goals cannot be overstated. Without clear goals, you might find yourself drifting without a sense of purpose. Goals give you something to strive for and help you measure your progress. They also keep you motivated and accountable.

There are two types of financial goals: short-term and long-term. Short-term goals are things you want to achieve within the next year or two, like saving for a vacation or paying off a credit card. Long-term goals are things you want to achieve in the next five, ten, or even twenty years, like buying a house or retiring comfortably.

Prioritizing your financial goals is essential. Not all goals are equally important, and you may need to focus on some before others. Start by listing all your goals, then rank them in order of importance. This will help you allocate your resources effectively and make progress on the most critical goals first.

One effective way to set financial goals is to use the SMART framework. SMART goals are Specific, Measurable, Achievable, Relevant, and Time-bound. This means your goals should be clear and specific, include a way to measure your progress, be realistic and attainable, align with your overall financial picture, and have a deadline for completion.

For example, instead of saying you want to save money, set a SMART goal like, "I want to save $5,000 for a down payment on a car in the next 12 months." This goal is specific (saving $5,000), measurable (you can track your savings), achievable (it's a realistic amount), relevant (it aligns with your need for a car), and time-bound (within 12 months).

Setting realistic financial goals is crucial. While it's good to aim high, setting goals that are too ambitious can lead to frustration and disappointment. Consider your current financial situation, income, and expenses when setting your goals. It's better to set smaller, achievable goals and build on your success over time.

Common financial goals include saving for emergencies, paying off debt, saving for retirement, and planning for major life events like buying a house or starting a family. Each of these goals requires careful planning and a clear strategy for achieving them.

When setting goals for saving and investing, it's essential to consider both your short-term and long-term needs. Short-term savings might be for things like a vacation or a new appliance, while long-term savings might be for retirement or a child's education. Balancing these needs requires careful planning and discipline.

Planning for major life events is an essential part of financial goal setting. Whether you're buying a house, getting married, or starting a family, these events can have a significant impact on your finances. Setting clear goals and planning ahead can help you manage these expenses without going into debt.

Debt reduction is another common financial goal. Whether you have credit card debt, student loans, or a mortgage, reducing your debt can free up resources for other goals. Develop a clear plan for paying off your debt, starting with the highest interest rates first.

Retirement planning should also be a priority. The earlier you start saving for retirement, the more time your money has to grow. Set clear goals for how much you want to save and develop a strategy for reaching those goals. Consider factors like your desired retirement age, lifestyle, and expected expenses.

As you work towards your financial goals, it's essential to stay flexible. Life is unpredictable, and your goals may need to change as your circumstances do. Be prepared to adjust your goals and your plan as needed, and don't be discouraged if you encounter setbacks. The key is to stay focused and keep moving forward.

Milestones can help you stay motivated and measure your progress. Break your larger goals into smaller, manageable steps, and celebrate your achievements along the way. This can give you a sense of accomplishment and keep you motivated to continue working towards your goals.

There are many tools and resources available to help you set and achieve your financial goals. From budgeting apps to financial planners, these tools can provide guidance, support, and accountability. Explore different options and find the ones that work best for you.

Flexibility is key in goal setting. Your financial situation and priorities may change over time, and your goals should reflect these changes. Regularly review your goals and adjust them as needed to ensure they remain relevant and achievable.

Achieving your financial goals can be challenging, but it's also incredibly rewarding. The satisfaction of reaching a goal and the financial security that comes with it are well worth the effort. Stay focused, stay motivated, and keep your eyes on the prize.

In the next chapter, we'll dive into budgeting for success. A budget is a powerful tool that can help you achieve your financial goals by managing your income and expenses effectively. Let's explore how to create a budget that works for you.

Chapter 3: Budgeting for Success

Budgeting is like creating a game plan for your money. It's a way to ensure you're spending and saving in a way that aligns with your financial goals. A budget helps you live within your means, avoid debt, and save for the things that matter most to you. It's an essential tool for financial success.

The first step in budgeting is understanding why it's important. A budget gives you control over your money and helps you make informed decisions about how to use it. It can reduce financial stress and provide a clear path to achieving your goals. Without a budget, it's easy to overspend and lose track of where your money is going.

There are different types of budgets, and finding the right one for you is crucial. Some people prefer a zero-based budget, where every dollar is allocated to a specific purpose. Others prefer a 50/30/20 budget, where 50% of your income goes to necessities, 30% to wants, and 20% to savings and debt repayment. The key is to find a system that works for you and stick to it.

Creating a budget involves several steps. Start by tracking your income and expenses for a month to get a clear picture of your financial situation. This will help you identify areas where you can cut back and save more. Next, set clear spending limits for each category, such as housing, food, transportation, and entertainment. Make sure to include savings and debt repayment in your budget.

Understanding your income and expenses is the foundation of a successful budget. Your income includes all the money you earn, such as your salary, bonuses, and any other sources of income. Your expenses include everything you spend money on, from rent and groceries to entertainment and dining out. By tracking these, you can see where your money is going and make adjustments as needed.

Fixed expenses are costs that stay the same each month, like rent or a car payment. Variable expenses are costs that can change, like groceries or utility bills.

Understanding the difference between these types of expenses can help you create a more accurate budget.

Tracking your expenses is an essential part of budgeting. This can be done using a spreadsheet, a budgeting app, or even a notebook. The key is to be consistent and track every expense, no matter how small. This will help you see where your money is going and identify areas where you can cut back.

Categorizing your expenses can make budgeting easier. Common categories include housing, transportation, food, entertainment, and savings. By grouping similar expenses together, you can see how much you're spending in each area and make adjustments as needed.

Setting spending limits is an important part of budgeting. This involves deciding how much you're willing to spend in each category and sticking to those limits. It's important to be realistic and make sure your spending limits reflect your actual expenses.

A balanced budget is one where your income equals your expenses. This means you're not spending more than you earn and you're living within your means. If your expenses are higher than your income, you'll need to make adjustments to bring them into balance.

Sticking to your budget can be challenging, but it's essential for financial success. This involves being disciplined and making sure you're not overspending in any category. It may require making some sacrifices, but the rewards are well worth it.

Common budgeting mistakes include underestimating expenses, not tracking spending, and failing to adjust the budget as needed. Avoiding these pitfalls requires being realistic about your expenses, tracking every penny, and regularly reviewing your budget to make sure it still works for you.

Adjusting your budget over time is crucial. Your financial situation and goals may change, and your budget should reflect these changes. Regularly review your budget and make any necessary adjustments to ensure it remains relevant and effective.

Technology can be a valuable tool in budgeting. There are many apps and online tools available that can help you track your income and expenses, set spending limits, and monitor your progress. These tools can make budgeting easier and more convenient.

Involving your family in budgeting can help ensure everyone's on the same page. This can involve setting family financial goals, discussing the budget, and working together to stick to it. By involving everyone, you can create a sense of accountability and teamwork.

Budgeting for irregular income can be challenging, but it's possible. This involves setting a baseline budget for your essential expenses and adjusting it based on your actual income each month. It's important to prioritize saving and avoid overspending during high-income months.

Regular budget reviews are essential. Set aside time each month to review your budget, track your progress, and make any necessary adjustments. This can help you stay on track and ensure your budget remains effective.

Case studies of successful budgeting can provide valuable insights and inspiration. Learn from others who have successfully managed their money and achieved their financial goals. Their stories can provide motivation and practical tips for your own budgeting journey.

Handling budget failures is part of the process. If you find yourself overspending or struggling to stick to your budget, don't get discouraged. Analyze what went wrong, make adjustments, and get back on track. Remember, budgeting is a learning process.

The impact of budgeting on your financial health cannot be overstated. A well-crafted budget can help you live within your means, avoid debt, save for your goals, and achieve financial security. It's a powerful tool that can transform your financial life.

Budgeting is not just about cutting back; it's about making conscious choices with your money. It's about prioritizing what's important to you and making sure your spending reflects your values and goals. With a budget, you can create a financial plan that works for you and helps you achieve your dreams.

In the next chapter, we'll explore the importance of building an emergency fund. This is a crucial step in your financial plan that can provide a safety net for unexpected expenses and help you stay on track with your financial goals.

Chapter 4: Building an Emergency Fund

An emergency fund is like a financial safety net. It's money set aside specifically for unexpected expenses, like car repairs, medical bills, or a sudden job loss. Having an emergency fund can provide peace of mind and protect you from going into debt when life throws you a curveball.

The importance of an emergency fund cannot be overstated. Without one, a single unexpected expense can derail your financial plan and force you to rely on credit cards or loans. An emergency fund gives you the flexibility to handle life's surprises without financial stress.

Determining how much to save in your emergency fund depends on your personal situation. A common recommendation is to save three to six months' worth of living expenses. This amount can provide a cushion to cover your essential expenses if you lose your job or face another financial emergency.

Building an emergency fund involves several steps. Start by setting a savings goal based on your monthly expenses. Next, create a plan to save a specific amount each month until you reach your goal. It's important to prioritize your emergency fund savings and make it a regular part of your budget.

Choosing where to keep your emergency fund is also important. It should be easily accessible in case of an emergency, but not so accessible that you're tempted to dip into it for non-emergencies. A high-yield savings account is a good option because it offers liquidity and earns interest.

Prioritizing your emergency fund savings means making it a top priority in your budget. This might involve cutting back on discretionary spending or finding ways to increase your income. The key is to make consistent progress towards your savings goal.

The role of an emergency fund in your financial plan is crucial. It provides a buffer that allows you to handle unexpected expenses without derailing your financial goals. This can give you peace of mind and a sense of financial security.

An emergency fund is different from a regular savings account. While both are important, an emergency fund is specifically for unexpected expenses, while a savings account can be for planned expenses like a vacation or a new appliance. Keeping these funds separate can help you stay disciplined.

There are several tips for saving for an emergency fund. Start small and gradually increase your savings over time. Automate your savings to make it easier and more consistent. Look for ways to cut back on non-essential expenses and redirect that money to your emergency fund.

Building an emergency fund can be challenging, especially if you're on a tight budget. The key is to stay focused and make consistent progress, even if it's small. Every little bit adds up over time, and the peace of mind it provides is worth the effort.

Using your emergency fund wisely is crucial. Only dip into it for true emergencies, like unexpected medical bills or car repairs. Avoid using it for non-essential expenses, and replenish it as soon as possible after you use it.

Replenishing your emergency fund is important. After using it for an emergency, make it a priority to rebuild your fund to its target amount. This ensures you always have a safety net in place.

Case studies of successful emergency fund savings can provide valuable insights and motivation. Learn from others who have built and used their emergency funds effectively. Their stories can provide practical tips and inspiration for your own savings journey.

The impact of an emergency fund on financial security is significant. It provides a buffer that allows you to handle unexpected expenses without going into debt. This can reduce financial stress and give you peace of mind.

Avoiding the temptation to dip into your emergency fund for non-emergencies is crucial. This requires discipline and a clear understanding of what constitutes an emergency. By keeping your fund separate and using it only for true emergencies, you can ensure it's there when you need it.

Building an emergency fund on a tight budget requires creativity and discipline. Look for ways to cut back on non-essential expenses, increase your income, and redirect that money to your emergency fund. Stay focused and make consistent progress, even if it's small.

Starting small is key when building an emergency fund. Don't get discouraged if you can't save a large amount right away. Every little bit adds up over time, and the important thing is to make consistent progress towards your goal.

Emergency fund strategies can vary depending on your income level. Higher-income individuals might be able to save more quickly, while lower-income individuals might need to focus on smaller, more manageable savings goals. The key is to find a strategy that works for you and stick to it.

Staying motivated to save for an emergency fund can be challenging, but it's essential. Remind yourself of the peace of mind and financial security it provides. Set small milestones and celebrate your progress along the way.

The impact of lifestyle choices on emergency fund savings is significant. By making conscious choices about how you spend and save your money, you can build a strong emergency fund and achieve your financial goals. This requires discipline and a clear understanding of your priorities.

Educating your family about the importance of an emergency fund can help ensure everyone's on the same page. Discuss your savings goals, the importance of having a safety net, and how everyone can contribute to building and maintaining the fund.

The long-term benefits of an emergency fund are substantial. It provides a financial safety net that can protect you from unexpected expenses and reduce financial stress. By making it a priority and staying disciplined, you can build a fund that provides peace of mind and financial security.

Next, we'll explore how to manage and reduce debt. Debt can be a significant obstacle to achieving your financial goals, but with the right strategies, you can take control and eliminate it.

Chapter 5: Managing and Reducing Debt

Debt is like a heavy backpack you're carrying on a hike. It can weigh you down and make it harder to reach your destination. Managing and reducing debt is essential for achieving your financial goals and gaining financial freedom. Understanding different types of debt is the first step in managing it effectively.

There are many types of debt, including credit card debt, student loans, mortgages, and car loans. Each type has its terms, interest rates, and repayment options. Understanding these differences is crucial for developing a strategy to manage and reduce your debt.

Not all debt is created equal. Some debt, like a mortgage, can be considered good debt because it helps you build wealth over time. Other debt, like credit card debt, is considered bad debt because it has high-interest rates and doesn't provide long-term value. Understanding the difference between good and bad debt can help you prioritize your repayment efforts.

The impact of debt on your financial health can be significant. High levels of debt can lead to financial stress, limit your ability to save and invest, and reduce your overall financial flexibility. Managing and reducing your debt is crucial for improving your financial health and achieving your goals.

Managing debt involves several steps. Start by assessing your total debt, including all your loans and credit card balances. Next, prioritize your debts based on interest rates and repayment terms. Develop a clear plan to pay off your highest-interest debts first, while making minimum payments on the rest.

Prioritizing debt repayment is essential. Focus on paying off high-interest debt first, as it costs you the most over time. Once you've paid off your high-interest debts, you can redirect those payments to other debts, creating a snowball effect that accelerates your debt reduction efforts.

There are several debt repayment strategies you can use. The snowball method involves paying off your smallest debts first, which can provide a sense of accomplishment and motivation to keep going. The avalanche method involves paying off your highest-interest debts first, which can save you the most money in the long run.

Staying motivated to pay off debt can be challenging, but it's essential for success. Celebrate your progress along the way, set small milestones, and remind yourself of the benefits of being debt-free. Staying focused and disciplined will help you stay on track.

Common mistakes in debt repayment include not prioritizing high-interest debt, missing payments, and accumulating new debt. Avoiding these pitfalls requires a clear plan, consistent effort, and a commitment to reducing your debt.

Your credit score plays a significant role in debt management. A higher credit score can help you qualify for lower interest rates and better loan terms, which can save you money over time. Understanding how your credit score is calculated and taking steps to improve it can help you manage your debt more effectively.

Improving your credit score involves several steps. Pay your bills on time, reduce your credit card balances, and avoid opening new credit accounts. Regularly review your credit report for errors and take steps to correct them. Over time, these efforts can improve your credit score and help you manage your debt.

Interest rates have a significant impact on your debt. Higher interest rates mean higher monthly payments and more money spent on interest over time. Understanding how interest rates work and finding ways to reduce them, such as refinancing or consolidating debt, can help you manage your debt more effectively.

Negotiating with creditors can be a valuable strategy for managing debt. If you're struggling to make payments, contact your creditors to discuss your options. They may be willing to lower your interest rates, reduce your monthly payments, or offer a settlement. Being proactive and communicating with your creditors can help you find solutions.

Debt consolidation is another option for managing debt. This involves combining multiple debts into a single loan with a lower interest rate. While it won't reduce your total debt, it can simplify your payments and reduce your interest costs. Consider the pros and cons of debt consolidation and explore your options.

Avoiding new debt is crucial for reducing your overall debt load. This involves being disciplined with your spending, avoiding unnecessary purchases, and focusing on your financial goals. By living within your means and prioritizing debt repayment, you can avoid accumulating new debt.

Budgeting plays a significant role in debt reduction. By creating a realistic budget and sticking to it, you can free up resources to pay off your debt more quickly. Regularly review your budget and make adjustments as needed to stay on track with your debt repayment goals.

Case studies of successful debt management can provide valuable insights and inspiration. Learn from others who have successfully reduced their debt and achieved financial freedom. Their stories can provide practical tips and motivation for your own debt reduction journey.

The emotional impact of debt can be significant. Debt-related stress can affect your mental and physical health, relationships, and overall well-being. Managing and reducing your debt can improve your quality of life and provide a sense of financial security.

Handling debt-related stress involves several strategies. Develop a clear plan for managing your debt, stay focused on your goals, and seek support from friends, family, or a financial advisor. Practicing self-care and stress management techniques can also help you cope with debt-related stress.

The benefits of being debt-free are substantial. Without debt, you have more financial flexibility, can save and invest more, and achieve your financial goals more easily. The sense of accomplishment and financial security that comes with being debt-free is worth the effort.

Next, we'll explore the importance of saving for the future. Saving is a crucial part of your financial plan that can help you achieve your goals and build wealth over time.

Chapter 6: Saving for the Future

Saving money is like planting seeds in a garden. Over time, those seeds grow into plants that provide food, beauty, and shade. Similarly, saving money allows you to build wealth, achieve your goals, and provide financial security for the future. It's an essential part of any financial plan.

The importance of saving for the future cannot be overstated. It provides a cushion for unexpected expenses, helps you achieve your financial goals, and ensures you have money for major life events and retirement. Without savings, you're more vulnerable to financial setbacks and less able to take advantage of opportunities.

There are two main types of savings: short-term and long-term. Short-term savings are for goals you want to achieve within the next year or two, like a vacation or a new appliance. Long-term savings are for goals that are further down the road, like buying a house or retiring comfortably. Both types of savings are important and require careful planning.

Setting savings goals is an essential part of saving for the future. Your goals should be specific, measurable, achievable, relevant, and time-bound. This means you need to be clear about what you want to achieve, how you'll measure your progress, ensure the goals are attainable, make sure they align with your overall financial picture, and set a timeline for achieving them.

There are different types of savings accounts, each with its benefits and limitations. A regular savings account is a good place to start because it's easily accessible and earns interest. A high-yield savings account offers higher interest rates, which can help your savings grow faster. Money market accounts and certificates of deposit (CDs) are other options that offer higher returns but may have restrictions on withdrawals.

The role of interest rates in savings is significant. Higher interest rates mean your money grows faster, while lower interest rates mean it grows more slowly.

Understanding how interest rates work and choosing accounts with higher rates can help you maximize your savings.

There are several tips for increasing your savings. Start by setting a savings goal and creating a plan to achieve it. Automate your savings to make it easier and more consistent. Look for ways to cut back on non-essential expenses and redirect that money to your savings. Regularly review your progress and make adjustments as needed.

The impact of compound interest on savings is substantial. Compound interest is the interest you earn on both your initial savings and the interest you've already earned. Over time, this can significantly increase your savings. The earlier you start saving, the more time your money has to grow.

Automating your savings is a simple and effective way to ensure you save consistently. Set up automatic transfers from your checking account to your savings account each month. This way, you can save without even thinking about it.

Saving for retirement is a crucial part of your financial plan. There are different types of retirement accounts, each with its benefits and limitations. These include 401(k) plans, individual retirement accounts (IRAs), and Roth IRAs. Understanding these options can help you make informed decisions about your retirement savings.

Choosing the right retirement account depends on your financial situation and goals. A 401(k) plan, offered by many employers, allows you to save money pre-tax, which can reduce your taxable income. IRAs and Roth IRAs offer different tax advantages and can be good options if you don't have access to a 401(k).

Maximizing your retirement savings involves several strategies. Take advantage of employer matching contributions if available, as this is essentially free money. Contribute the maximum amount allowed each year to take advantage of tax benefits. Diversify your investments to reduce risk and increase potential returns.

Balancing saving and investing is essential for long-term financial success. While saving provides a safety net, investing can help your money grow faster and achieve your long-term goals. Understanding the difference between saving and investing and finding the right balance is crucial.

Inflation can erode the value of your savings over time. This is why it's important to not only save but also invest some of your money to keep up with or outpace inflation. By doing so, you can maintain your purchasing power and achieve your financial goals.

Saving for major life events, like buying a house or starting a family, requires careful planning. Set clear goals, create a savings plan, and start saving as early as possible. This can help you avoid debt and ensure you have the money you need when the time comes.

Staying motivated to save can be challenging, but it's essential for achieving your goals. Set small milestones and celebrate your progress along the way. Remind yourself of the benefits of saving and the financial security it provides. Stay focused and keep your eyes on the prize.

Common challenges in saving include unexpected expenses, lack of discipline, and competing financial priorities. Overcoming these challenges requires a clear plan, consistent effort, and a commitment to your goals. By staying focused and disciplined, you can build a strong savings habit.

The role of discipline in saving is crucial. It requires making conscious choices about how you spend and save your money, staying focused on your goals, and avoiding the temptation to dip into your savings for non-essential expenses. By staying disciplined, you can build a strong financial foundation.

Case studies of successful saving can provide valuable insights and motivation. Learn from others who have successfully built their savings and achieved their financial goals. Their stories can provide practical tips and inspiration for your own savings journey.

The benefits of a strong savings habit are substantial. It provides financial security, allows you to achieve your goals, and gives you the flexibility to handle unexpected expenses. By making saving a priority and staying disciplined, you can build a strong financial foundation.

Next, we'll explore the importance of investing wisely. Investing is a crucial part of your financial plan that can help you build wealth and achieve your long-term goals.

Chapter 7: Investing Wisely

Investing is like planting a tree. With time, care, and patience, it grows and bears fruit. Similarly, investing allows your money to grow and provides financial benefits over time. It's a crucial part of any financial plan and can help you achieve your long-term goals.

The importance of investing cannot be overstated. It allows your money to work for you and grow faster than it would in a savings account. Investing can help you build wealth, achieve your financial goals, and provide financial security for the future.

There are many types of investments, each with its risks and potential returns. These include stocks, bonds, mutual funds, exchange-traded funds (ETFs), real estate, and more. Understanding these different options is crucial for making informed investment decisions.

The role of risk in investing is significant. All investments come with some level of risk, and understanding your risk tolerance is essential. This involves assessing how much risk you're willing to take and how it aligns with your financial goals and time horizon.

Assessing your risk tolerance involves several factors. Consider your financial goals, time horizon, and comfort level with market fluctuations. It's important to find a balance between risk and return that aligns with your overall financial picture.

Starting to invest involves several steps. First, set clear investment goals based on your financial objectives and time horizon. Next, choose the right investments that align with your risk tolerance and goals. Finally, create a diversified investment portfolio to reduce risk and increase potential returns.

Diversification is a key strategy in investing. It involves spreading your investments across different asset classes, such as stocks, bonds, and real estate, to reduce risk. By diversifying your portfolio, you can minimize the impact of any single investment's performance on your overall portfolio.

Building an investment portfolio involves selecting a mix of investments that align with your financial goals and risk tolerance. This might include a combination of stocks for growth, bonds for stability, and real estate for income. Regularly review and adjust your portfolio to ensure it remains aligned with your goals.

Stocks are a common investment option that offers the potential for high returns but also comes with higher risk. Investing in stocks involves buying shares of a company and benefiting from its growth and profitability. It's important to research and choose stocks wisely.

Bonds are another investment option that offers lower risk and stable returns. When you buy a bond, you're essentially lending money to a company or government, and they pay you interest in return. Bonds can provide a steady income and help balance the risk in your portfolio.

Mutual funds and ETFs are investment options that pool money from many investors to buy a diversified portfolio of stocks, bonds, or other assets. They offer diversification and professional management, making them a good option for beginner investors.

Real estate can be a valuable part of an investment portfolio. It offers the potential for rental income and long-term appreciation. Investing in real estate involves buying properties, either directly or through real estate investment trusts (REITs), and benefiting from their growth and income.

Taxes can have a significant impact on your investment returns. Understanding the tax implications of your investments and finding ways to minimize taxes can help you keep more of your money. Consider tax-advantaged accounts like IRAs and 401(k)s to reduce your tax burden.

Minimizing investment taxes involves several strategies. These include holding investments for the long term to benefit from lower capital gains rates, using tax-advantaged accounts, and strategically selling investments to offset gains and losses.

Retirement accounts play a crucial role in investing. These accounts, like 401(k)s and IRAs, offer tax benefits that can help your money grow faster. Understanding these options and maximizing your contributions can significantly impact your retirement savings.

Balancing saving and investing is essential for long-term financial success. While saving provides a safety net, investing can help your money grow faster and achieve your long-term goals. Understanding the difference between saving and investing and finding the right balance is crucial.

Common investing mistakes include not diversifying, trying to time the market, and letting emotions drive investment decisions. Avoiding these pitfalls requires a clear investment plan, consistent effort, and a commitment to long-term goals.

The role of a financial advisor in investing can be valuable. They can provide objective advice, help you develop a comprehensive investment plan, and keep you accountable. If you're new to investing or unsure about your options, a financial advisor can provide guidance and support.

Case studies of successful investing can provide valuable insights and motivation. Learn from others who have successfully built their investment portfolios and achieved their financial goals. Their stories can provide practical tips and inspiration for your own investing journey.

Market volatility is a natural part of investing. Understanding how to navigate market ups and downs is crucial for long-term success. Stay focused on your goals, avoid making impulsive decisions, and remember that investing is a marathon, not a sprint.

Staying informed about investment opportunities is essential. Regularly review your investments, stay updated on market trends, and seek out new opportunities that align with your goals. Education and research are key components of successful investing.

In the next chapter, we'll explore the importance of planning for retirement. Retirement planning is a crucial part of your financial plan that can help you achieve financial security and enjoy your golden years.

Chapter 8: Planning for Retirement

Planning for retirement is like preparing for a long vacation. You need to decide where you want to go, how long you'll stay, and what you'll do while you're there. Similarly, retirement planning involves setting goals, estimating how much money you'll need, and developing a strategy to achieve those goals.

The importance of retirement planning cannot be overstated. It ensures you have enough money to live comfortably in your golden years and provides financial security. Without a clear retirement plan, you risk running out of money and facing financial difficulties in your later years.

There are different types of retirement plans, each with its benefits and limitations. These include 401(k) plans, individual retirement accounts (IRAs), and Roth IRAs. Understanding these options is crucial for making informed decisions about your retirement savings.

Choosing the right retirement plan depends on your financial situation and goals. A 401(k) plan, offered by many employers, allows you to save money pre-tax, which can reduce your taxable income. IRAs and Roth IRAs offer different tax advantages and can be good options if you don't have access to a 401(k).

Steps to create a retirement plan involve several key actions. First, set clear retirement goals based on your desired lifestyle and estimated expenses. Next, estimate how much money you'll need to save to achieve those goals. Finally, develop a strategy to reach your savings targets, including contributions to retirement accounts and investments.

The role of savings in retirement planning is significant. Regularly contributing to retirement accounts and maximizing your savings can help you build a substantial nest egg. This involves making consistent contributions, taking advantage of employer matching, and prioritizing retirement savings in your budget.

Determining how much to save for retirement can be challenging. It involves estimating your future expenses, including housing, healthcare, and leisure activities. Consider factors like inflation and potential changes in your lifestyle. A common rule of thumb is to aim for 70-80% of your pre-retirement income.

The impact of lifestyle on retirement savings is substantial. Your desired retirement lifestyle will significantly influence how much you need to save. Whether you plan to travel the world or live a modest life at home, it's important to align your savings goals with your retirement vision.

Maximizing retirement savings involves several strategies. Take advantage of employer matching contributions if available, as this is essentially free money. Contribute the maximum amount allowed each year to take advantage of tax benefits. Diversify your investments to reduce risk and increase potential returns.

Employer-sponsored retirement plans play a crucial role in retirement savings. Many employers offer 401(k) plans with matching contributions. Understanding the details of your employer's plan, including contribution limits and matching policies, can help you make the most of this benefit.

Understanding Social Security benefits is an essential part of retirement planning. Social Security can provide a significant portion of your retirement income, but it's important to understand how benefits are calculated and the best time to start receiving them. Delaying benefits can increase your monthly payments.

Maximizing Social Security benefits involves several strategies. Delaying benefits until full retirement age or beyond can increase your monthly payments. Understanding how your benefits are calculated and planning your retirement accordingly can help you maximize your Social Security income.

Healthcare costs can have a significant impact on your retirement savings. It's important to plan for these expenses, including insurance premiums, out-of-pocket costs, and long-term care. Consider options like Medicare and supplemental insurance to cover these costs.

Planning for healthcare expenses involves estimating your future healthcare needs and costs. This includes regular medical expenses, potential long-term care, and insurance premiums. Setting aside funds specifically for healthcare can help ensure you have the resources you need.

Long-term care insurance can be a valuable part of your retirement plan. It helps cover the costs of care that aren't covered by regular health insurance, such as assistance with daily activities. Choosing the right policy involves understanding the coverage options and costs.

Choosing the right long-term care insurance involves several factors. Consider the types of care covered, the daily benefit amount, the benefit period, and the cost of the policy. Understanding these details can help you select a policy that meets your needs and budget.

Estate planning is an essential part of retirement planning. It involves creating a plan for how your assets will be distributed after your death. This includes creating a will, setting up trusts, and designating beneficiaries. Proper estate planning can help ensure your wishes are carried out and reduce the tax burden on your heirs.

Creating an estate plan involves several steps. Start by taking an inventory of your assets and deciding how you want them distributed. Create a will to outline your wishes, and consider setting up trusts to protect your assets and provide for your heirs. Designate beneficiaries for your retirement accounts and insurance policies.

Wills and trusts play a crucial role in estate planning. A will outlines how your assets will be distributed after your death, while trusts can help protect your assets and provide for your heirs. Understanding the differences and benefits of each can help you create a comprehensive estate plan.

Choosing the right estate planning tools depends on your financial situation and goals. A simple will might be sufficient for some, while others may benefit from more complex arrangements like trusts. Consulting with an estate planning attorney can help you make informed decisions.

Taxes can have a significant impact on your retirement savings. Understanding the tax implications of your retirement accounts and finding ways to minimize taxes can help you keep more of your money. Consider tax-advantaged accounts like IRAs and 401(k)s to reduce your tax burden.

Minimizing retirement taxes involves several strategies. These include using tax-advantaged accounts, timing your withdrawals to minimize tax impacts, and considering the tax implications of your estate plan. Working with a financial advisor can help you develop a tax-efficient retirement strategy.

Case studies of successful retirement planning can provide valuable insights and motivation. Learn from others who have successfully planned for retirement and achieved financial security. Their stories can provide practical tips and inspiration for your own retirement journey.

Common retirement planning mistakes include not saving enough, underestimating expenses, and failing to plan for healthcare costs. Avoiding these pitfalls requires a clear plan, consistent effort, and a commitment to your goals. By staying focused and disciplined, you can achieve a financially secure retirement.

Next, we'll explore the importance of protecting your wealth. Protecting your wealth involves strategies to safeguard your assets and ensure your financial security. Let's dive into the different ways to protect your hard-earned money and secure your financial future.

Chapter 9: Protecting Your Wealth

Protecting your wealth is like building a fortress around your finances. It involves strategies to safeguard your assets and ensure your financial security. This is an essential part of any comprehensive financial plan, as it helps you preserve what you've worked so hard to build.

The importance of protecting your wealth cannot be overstated. Without proper protection, your assets are vulnerable to risks like lawsuits, accidents, and natural disasters. By implementing effective protection strategies, you can mitigate these risks and ensure your financial security.

There are different types of insurance that can help protect your wealth. These include life insurance, health insurance, disability insurance, and property insurance. Each type of insurance plays a crucial role in safeguarding your financial well-being.

Life insurance is essential for protecting your family's financial security. It provides a death benefit to your beneficiaries in the event of your death. This can help cover expenses like funeral costs, outstanding debts, and living expenses for your loved ones.

Choosing the right life insurance policy involves several factors. Consider the amount of coverage you need, the type of policy (term or permanent), and the cost of premiums. Understanding these details can help you select a policy that meets your needs and budget.

Disability insurance is another important type of coverage. It provides income replacement if you're unable to work due to illness or injury. This can help ensure you have the resources you need to cover your expenses and maintain your standard of living.

Choosing the right disability insurance involves understanding the types of coverage available, the benefit amount, and the cost of premiums. Consider factors like your occupation, income, and financial obligations when selecting a policy.

Health insurance is crucial for protecting your wealth. Medical expenses can be significant, and without proper coverage, they can quickly deplete your savings. Understanding your health insurance options and choosing the right plan can help you manage these costs.

Choosing the right health insurance involves several factors. Consider the types of coverage offered, the cost of premiums and out-of-pocket expenses, and the network of providers. Understanding these details can help you select a plan that meets your needs and budget.

Property insurance, including homeowners and renters insurance, protects your assets from risks like fire, theft, and natural disasters. This coverage can help you repair or replace your property if it's damaged or destroyed.

Choosing the right property insurance involves understanding the types of coverage available, the cost of premiums, and the deductible amount. Consider factors like the value of your property, the risks in your area, and your financial situation when selecting a policy.

Liability insurance is another important type of coverage. It protects you from financial loss if you're held responsible for injury or damage to others. This coverage can help cover legal fees, medical expenses, and damages awarded in a lawsuit.

Choosing the right liability insurance involves understanding the types of coverage available, the cost of premiums, and the coverage limits. Consider factors like your assets, lifestyle, and potential risks when selecting a policy.

Lawsuits can pose a significant risk to your wealth. If you're sued and found liable for damages, you could face substantial financial losses. Implementing asset protection strategies can help mitigate this risk and ensure your financial security.

Asset protection strategies involve several approaches. These include using legal structures like trusts and limited liability companies (LLCs), purchasing appropriate insurance coverage, and keeping your personal and business finances separate. Understanding these strategies can help you safeguard your assets.

Choosing the right legal advisor is crucial for protecting your wealth. An experienced attorney can help you develop a comprehensive asset protection plan that addresses your specific needs and goals. Look for an advisor with expertise in estate planning, tax law, and asset protection.

Financial advisors can also play a valuable role in protecting your wealth. They can provide guidance on insurance coverage, asset protection strategies, and overall financial planning. Working with a qualified advisor can help you make informed decisions and ensure your financial security.

Case studies of successful wealth protection can provide valuable insights and motivation. Learn from others who have effectively safeguarded their assets and achieved financial security. Their stories can provide practical tips and inspiration for your own wealth protection efforts.

Common wealth protection mistakes include underestimating risks, failing to implement proper insurance coverage, and neglecting asset protection strategies. Avoiding these pitfalls requires a clear plan, consistent effort, and a commitment to safeguarding your wealth.

Avoiding wealth protection pitfalls involves several strategies. These include regularly reviewing your insurance coverage, updating your asset protection plan as needed, and working with qualified advisors. Staying proactive and vigilant can help you protect your wealth and ensure your financial security.

The impact of estate planning on wealth protection is significant. Proper estate planning can help you minimize taxes, protect your assets, and ensure your wishes are carried out. This involves creating a comprehensive plan that addresses your specific needs and goals.

Next, we'll explore the importance of regularly reviewing and adjusting your financial plan. Life is full of changes, and your financial plan should reflect these changes to stay effective and relevant. Let's dive into the steps to keep your financial plan on track.

Chapter 10: Reviewing and Adjusting Your Plan

Regularly reviewing and adjusting your financial plan is like tuning up a car. Just as a car needs regular maintenance to run smoothly, your financial plan needs periodic review and adjustments to stay effective. This ensures your plan remains aligned with your goals and adapts to changes in your life.

The importance of reviewing your financial plan cannot be overstated. Life is full of changes, from new jobs and growing families to health issues and unexpected expenses. Regularly reviewing your plan helps you stay on track and make necessary adjustments to keep moving towards your goals.

How often you should review your plan depends on your circumstances, but a good rule of thumb is to review it at least once a year. Major life events, like getting married, having a child, or changing jobs, may require more frequent reviews. Staying proactive ensures your plan remains relevant and effective.

Steps to review your financial plan involve several key actions. Start by assessing your current financial situation, including your income, expenses, debts, and assets. Next, evaluate your financial goals and determine if they need to be adjusted. Finally, review your budget, savings, investments, and insurance coverage to ensure they align with your goals.

Financial goals play a crucial role in plan review. As your life changes, your goals may need to be adjusted. For example, you might need to save more for your child's education, pay off debt faster, or increase your retirement savings. Regularly reviewing and adjusting your goals ensures they remain relevant and achievable.

Adjusting your goals over time is essential. Life is unpredictable, and your financial situation may change. Be prepared to adjust your goals and your plan as needed to reflect these changes. This might involve setting new goals, reprioritizing existing ones, or extending timelines.

The impact of life changes on your financial plan can be significant. Major events like getting married, having a child, or buying a house can affect your financial situation and goals. Regularly reviewing your plan helps you stay on track and make necessary adjustments to accommodate these changes.

Adjusting your plan for life changes involves several steps. Start by assessing the impact of the change on your finances. Next, adjust your budget, savings, and investments to reflect the new situation. Finally, update your goals and develop a strategy to achieve them.

Budgeting plays a significant role in plan review. Regularly reviewing your budget helps ensure it remains aligned with your goals and financial situation. This involves tracking your income and expenses, identifying areas for improvement, and making necessary adjustments to stay on track.

Adjusting your budget over time is crucial. Your financial situation and goals may change, and your budget should reflect these changes. Regularly review your budget and make any necessary adjustments to ensure it remains effective and relevant.

Debt management is another important aspect of plan review. Regularly reviewing your debt and developing strategies to reduce it can help you stay on track with your financial goals. This might involve adjusting your debt repayment plan, consolidating debt, or negotiating with creditors.

Managing and reducing debt during plan review involves several strategies. Prioritize high-interest debt, make consistent payments, and explore options for refinancing or consolidating debt. Staying focused and disciplined can help you reduce your debt and achieve your financial goals.

Saving plays a crucial role in plan review. Regularly reviewing your savings goals and progress helps ensure you stay on track and make necessary adjustments. This might involve increasing your savings rate, setting new goals, or reallocating funds to different accounts.

Increasing your savings over time is essential for achieving your financial goals. This involves making consistent contributions, taking advantage of employer matching, and prioritizing savings in your budget. Regularly reviewing and adjusting your savings plan can help you stay on track.

Investing is another key aspect of plan review. Regularly reviewing your investments helps ensure they remain aligned with your goals and risk tolerance. This involves assessing your portfolio, making necessary adjustments, and staying informed about market trends.

Adjusting your investments over time is crucial. As your financial situation and goals change, your investment strategy may need to be updated. Regularly review your portfolio and make necessary adjustments to ensure it remains effective and aligned with your goals.

Retirement planning plays a significant role in plan review. Regularly reviewing your retirement goals and progress helps ensure you stay on track and make necessary adjustments. This might involve increasing your contributions, reassessing your retirement age, or adjusting your investment strategy.

Adjusting your retirement plan over time is essential for achieving your retirement goals. This involves regularly reviewing your savings, investments, and overall strategy to ensure it remains aligned with your goals and financial situation. Staying proactive can help you build a secure retirement.

Taxes can have a significant impact on your financial plan. Regularly reviewing your tax situation and finding ways to minimize taxes can help you keep more of your money. This involves understanding the tax implications of your savings, investments, and estate plan.

Minimizing taxes during plan review involves several strategies. These include using tax-advantaged accounts, timing your withdrawals to minimize tax impacts, and considering the tax implications of your estate plan. Working with a financial advisor can help you develop a tax-efficient strategy.

Insurance plays a crucial role in plan review. Regularly reviewing your insurance coverage helps ensure you have the right protection for your financial situation and goals. This involves assessing your life, health, disability, and property insurance and making necessary adjustments.

Adjusting your insurance over time is essential for protecting your wealth. As your life changes, your insurance needs may change as well. Regularly review your coverage and make any necessary adjustments to ensure you remain protected.

Case studies of successful plan reviews can provide valuable insights and motivation. Learn from others who have effectively reviewed and adjusted their plans to stay on track with their financial goals. Their stories can provide practical tips and inspiration for your own plan review process.

Common plan review mistakes include not reviewing frequently enough, failing to adjust goals and strategies, and overlooking important aspects like insurance and taxes. Avoiding these pitfalls requires a clear plan, consistent effort, and a commitment to regularly reviewing and adjusting your plan.

Regularly reviewing and adjusting your financial plan is crucial for staying on track with your goals. It ensures your plan remains relevant, effective, and aligned with your financial situation. By staying proactive and making necessary adjustments, you can achieve your financial goals and build a secure financial future.

www.ingramcontent.com/pod-product-compliance
Lightning Source LLC
Chambersburg PA
CBHW072049230526
45479CB00009B/330